THE ART OF E-COMMERCE: MASTERING THE DROPSHIPPING BUSINESS

CHAPTER TITLES:

1. The Rise of E-commerce
2. Understanding Dropshipping
3. Finding Profitable Niche Markets
4. Setting Up Your Dropshipping Store
5. Sourcing Products and Suppliers
6. Creating an Effective Product Listing
7. Managing Inventory and Order Fulfillment
8. Optimizing Your Website for Conversions
9. Marketing Strategies for Dropshipping Success
10. Social Media Advertising and Influencer Marketing
11. Search Engine Optimization (SEO) for E-commerce
12. Email Marketing and Customer Retention
13. Customer Service and Handling Returns
14. Scaling Your Dropshipping Business
15. Legal Considerations and Future Trends

Book Introduction:

Welcome to "The Art of E-commerce: Mastering the Dropshipping Business." In this comprehensive guide, we will delve into the exciting world of dropshipping and equip you with the knowledge and skills needed to succeed in this rapidly growing industry.

CHAPTER 1: THE RISE OF E-COMMERCE

In recent years, e-commerce has experienced a monumental rise, revolutionizing the way people shop and do business. The convenience of online shopping, coupled with the vast array of products and services available, has attracted millions of customers worldwide. As a result, entrepreneurs have been drawn to the opportunities presented by this digital marketplace, leading to the rapid growth of dropshipping.

1.1 The Shifting Landscape

Traditional retail has faced significant challenges in keeping up with the fast-paced, ever-changing demands of consumers. Physical stores require substantial investments in inventory, storage space, and personnel, making it difficult for small businesses to compete on a level playing field. Moreover, geographical limitations often restrict their customer reach.

E-commerce has shattered these barriers, enabling businesses of all sizes to reach a global audience without the need for a physical storefront. The rise of reliable logistics networks and secure online payment systems has further facilitated this shift.

1.2 The Advantages of Dropshipping

Within the e-commerce realm, dropshipping has emerged as a popular business model due to its unique advantages. Unlike traditional retail, dropshipping eliminates the need for inventory management and order fulfillment. Instead, entrepreneurs act as intermediaries, connecting customers with suppliers who handle product storage, packaging, and shipping.

The primary benefit of dropshipping is its low barrier to entry. With minimal upfront investment, anyone can start an online store and begin selling products immediately. This has opened doors for aspiring entrepreneurs, allowing them to dip their toes into the world of e-commerce without the financial risks associated with traditional retail.

Additionally, dropshipping offers immense flexibility. Entrepreneurs can curate their product offerings, experiment with different niches, and easily pivot their businesses based on market trends and customer preferences. With a vast network of suppliers and an extensive range of products available, entrepreneurs have the freedom to cater to various customer demands.

1.3 The Impact on Consumers

For consumers, dropshipping brings numerous benefits as well. The convenience of online shopping means they can browse and purchase products from the comfort of their homes, at any time of the day. The vast selection of products from different suppliers provides them with unparalleled options and the ability to compare prices and quality easily.

Furthermore, dropshipping has led to competitive pricing in the e-commerce space. With multiple retailers selling the same products, businesses are compelled to offer attractive prices and incentives to capture customers. This has empowered consumers to make informed purchasing decisions while enjoying cost savings.

1.4 The Future of E-commerce and Dropshipping

As technology continues to advance, the future of e-commerce and dropshipping appears promising. Artificial intelligence (AI) and machine learning algorithms are being employed to personalize customer experiences and improve product recommendations. Augmented reality (AR) and virtual reality (VR) technologies are enhancing the online shopping experience, allowing customers to visualize products before making a purchase.

Moreover, the growth of mobile commerce, social commerce, and voice-activated assistants is expanding the avenues through which customers can engage with dropshipping businesses. These developments create exciting opportunities for entrepreneurs to reach and connect with their target audiences in innovative ways.

In the following chapters, we will delve deeper into the intricacies of dropshipping, providing you with invaluable knowledge and practical insights to master this art. Whether you are an aspiring entrepreneur looking to launch your first online store or an established e-commerce business owner seeking to enhance your dropshipping strategies, this book will equip you with the tools you need to succeed in the dynamic world of e-commerce.

CHAPTER 2: UNDERSTANDING DROPSHIPPING

2.1 The Dropshipping Process

To excel in the dropshipping business, it's crucial to understand the intricacies of the dropshipping process. Let's take a closer look at the key steps involved:

1. Customer Places an Order: The dropshipping process begins when a customer places an order on your online store.

2. Order Confirmation and Payment: Upon receiving the order, you'll send an order confirmation to the customer and collect payment for the product, including your profit margin.

3. Forwarding the Order to the Supplier: Once payment is confirmed, you'll forward the order details to the supplier who stocks the product.

4. Supplier Handles Packaging and Shipping: The supplier takes care of packaging the product and arranging its shipment directly to the customer. This relieves you of the burden of inventory management and fulfillment.

5. Shipment Tracking: Keep your customer informed by providing them with the shipment tracking information. This allows them to monitor the progress of their order.

6. Delivery to the Customer: The supplier delivers the product to the customer's designated address. It's essential to ensure that the delivery is prompt and the product arrives in good condition.

7. Customer Support: Throughout the process, you'll provide customer support, answering any inquiries, resolving issues, and ensuring a positive buying experience.

2.2 Benefits of the Dropshipping Model

Dropshipping offers several advantages that have contributed to its popularity among entrepreneurs. Let's explore some of the key benefits:

1. Lower Startup Costs: Compared to traditional retail, dropshipping requires minimal upfront investment. You don't need to purchase inventory or manage a physical store, reducing your initial financial risk.

2. Flexibility and Scalability: The dropshipping model allows you to easily scale your business. With a vast array of products available from various suppliers, you can expand your product offerings and cater to different market segments.

3. Reduced Operational Burden: By eliminating inventory management and fulfillment responsibilities, dropshipping frees up your time and resources. You can focus on marketing, customer service, and growing your business.

4. Location Independence: Dropshipping is not bound by geographical limitations. As long as you have a reliable internet connection, you can operate your business from anywhere in the world, providing you with the freedom and flexibility to work remotely.

5. Wide Product Selection: With access to a network of suppliers, you can offer an extensive range of products to your customers. This variety enables you to adapt to market trends and meet diverse customer demands.

2.3 Challenges and Considerations

While dropshipping presents numerous opportunities, it's essential to be aware of the challenges and considerations involved:

1. Supplier Reliability: Choosing reputable and reliable suppliers is crucial. Conduct thorough research, verify their reputation, and assess their product quality, shipping times, and customer service before partnering with them.

2. Competition: Dropshipping is a popular business model, and as a result, competition can be fierce. Differentiating your brand, finding unique products, and providing exceptional customer service are essential for standing out in the market.

3. Margins and Pricing: As an intermediary, your profit margins will depend on the price you set for the products. It's important to strike a balance between competitive pricing and maintaining healthy profit margins.

4. Inventory Management: While you don't have to manage physical inventory, staying on top of stock availability and

coordinating with suppliers is crucial to ensure smooth order fulfillment.

5. Customer Satisfaction: As the face of the business, providing excellent customer support is vital. Promptly addressing inquiries, handling returns or refunds, and ensuring a positive buying experience are key to building customer loyalty.

In the upcoming chapters, we'll delve into each aspect of the dropshipping process, providing you with strategies and best practices to overcome challenges and build a successful

dropshipping business. Get ready to equip yourself with the knowledge and skills necessary to master the art of dropshipping and thrive in the competitive e-commerce landscape.

CHAPTER 3: FINDING PROFITABLE NICHE MARKETS

3.1 The Importance of Niche Selection

In the world of dropshipping, finding a profitable niche market is crucial to your success. A niche refers to a specific segment of the market with unique needs and preferences. By targeting a niche, you can focus your efforts on a specific group of customers and tailor your products and marketing strategies to meet their specific demands. Here's why niche selection is important:

1. Reduced Competition: By targeting a niche, you can differentiate yourself from larger, more generalized retailers. A niche market allows you to carve out a specialized position, making it easier to attract and retain customers who are specifically interested in the products you offer.

2. Targeted Marketing: Understanding your niche audience enables you to create targeted marketing campaigns. You can tailor your messaging, advertising channels, and content to resonate with the unique needs and preferences of your niche customers. This increases the effectiveness of your marketing efforts and helps you connect with the right audience.

3. Higher Conversion Rates: When you cater to a specific niche,

you can provide products that precisely meet their needs. This leads to higher conversion rates as customers are more likely to purchase products that align with their specific requirements. By offering a focused product selection, you can build trust and loyalty within your niche market.

3.2 Identifying Profitable Niche Markets

Finding a profitable niche market requires research and analysis. Here are some steps to guide you in identifying potential niche markets:

1. Identify Your Interests and Passions: Start by exploring your own interests, hobbies, and areas of expertise. Passion for a particular subject will drive your motivation and make it easier to stay committed to your business in the long run.

2. Research Market Trends: Use online tools and platforms to research current market trends. Look for emerging industries, growing consumer interests, and untapped market segments. Pay attention to rising keywords and search volumes related to specific niches.

3. Assess Market Size and Competition: Evaluate the size of the potential niche market and the level of competition within it. A niche that is too small may limit your growth opportunities, while a niche that is oversaturated with competitors might make it difficult to stand out.

4. Analyze Customer Needs and Pain Points: Dive deep into understanding the needs, desires, and pain points of your target niche customers. Conduct surveys, read online forums and social media discussions, and engage with potential customers to gain insights into their specific requirements.

5. Validate Demand and Profitability: Use market research tools, keyword analysis, and competitor analysis to validate the demand and profitability of the niche. Look for indicators such as search volume, product demand, pricing trends, and customer reviews.

6. Consider Seasonality and Longevity: Evaluate the seasonality and long-term sustainability of the niche. Some niches may experience fluctuations in demand based on seasonal trends, while others offer more consistent demand throughout the year.

7. Test and Refine: Once you've identified a potential niche, test it by launching a small-scale campaign or pilot project. Collect data, analyze the results, and refine your approach based on customer feedback and market response.

Remember, the ideal niche market is one that aligns with your interests, has sufficient demand, and offers profitability potential. Take the time to conduct thorough research and choose a niche that you are passionate about and has room for growth.

In the next chapter, we'll delve into the process of setting up your dropshipping store, including selecting an e-commerce platform, domain registration, and designing your website to appeal to your niche audience. Stay tuned as we continue our journey to mastering the dropshipping business.

CHAPTER 4: SETTING UP YOUR DROPSHIPPING STORE

4.1 Choosing an E-commerce Platform

Selecting the right e-commerce platform is crucial for establishing a successful dropshipping store. The platform you choose will serve as the foundation for your online business, providing you with the tools and features necessary to manage your products, process orders, and optimize your store's performance. Consider the following factors when choosing an e-commerce platform:

1. Ease of Use: Look for a platform that is user-friendly and intuitive, especially if you're new to e-commerce. A simple interface and easy navigation will save you time and frustration when managing your store.

2. Dropshipping Integration: Ensure that the platform seamlessly integrates with dropshipping suppliers and automation tools. Look for built-in features or plugins that allow for easy product importing, inventory synchronization, and order fulfillment.

3. Customization Options: Your store should reflect your brand and appeal to your niche audience. Choose a platform that offers customization options for design, layout, and branding. This will

enable you to create a unique and visually appealing storefront.

4. Scalability: Consider the growth potential of your store and choose a platform that can accommodate your future needs. Look for scalability features such as the ability to handle a large number of products, high traffic volumes, and integrations with third-party apps.

5. Payment Gateway Options: Ensure that the platform supports popular payment gateways and offers a secure and seamless checkout experience for your customers. Multiple payment options will enhance convenience and trust for your buyers.

4.2 Domain Registration and Branding

Your domain name and branding play a crucial role in establishing your dropshipping store's identity. Here are some tips for domain registration and branding:

1. Choose a Memorable Domain Name: Select a domain name that is easy to remember, relevant to your niche, and reflects your brand identity. Keep it concise, avoid hyphens or numbers, and aim for a domain extension (.com, .net, etc.) that is widely recognized.

2. Branding Elements: Develop a cohesive branding strategy that includes a visually appealing logo, color scheme, and typography. Ensure that your branding elements align with your niche and appeal to your target audience.

3. Consistent Branding Across Channels: Maintain consistency in your branding across your website, social media profiles, and marketing materials. This will help create a strong and recognizable brand identity.

4.3 Designing Your Storefront

The design of your dropshipping store has a significant impact on user experience and conversion rates. Consider the following design principles when setting up your storefront:

1. Clean and User-Friendly Layout: Opt for a clean and clutter-free layout that guides visitors smoothly through your store. Make sure your navigation is intuitive, product categories are clearly displayed, and search functionality is easily accessible.

2. High-Quality Product Images: Use high-resolution product images that showcase your products from different angles. Ensure that the images are visually appealing and accurately represent the product.

3. Compelling Product Descriptions: Write compelling and informative product descriptions that highlight the features, benefits, and unique selling points of each item. Use persuasive language and incorporate relevant keywords for SEO purposes.

4. Mobile-Friendly Design: With the increasing use of smartphones for online shopping, it's essential to have a mobile-friendly design. Optimize your store's responsiveness and ensure that it provides a seamless browsing and purchasing experience on mobile devices.

5. Trust Signals and Social Proof: Incorporate trust signals, such as customer reviews, ratings, and security badges, to build trust and credibility with your potential buyers. Displaying social proof can significantly impact their purchasing decisions.

6. Clear Calls-to-Action: Use clear and prominent calls-to-action (CTAs) to guide visitors towards making a purchase. Strategically

place CTAs such as "Add to

Cart" or "Buy Now" buttons to encourage conversions.

By carefully selecting an e-commerce platform, registering a domain, and designing an appealing storefront, you lay the foundation for a successful dropshipping business. In the next chapter, we will explore effective product sourcing strategies and finding reliable suppliers to ensure a smooth and efficient fulfillment process. Stay tuned for more insights and guidance on mastering the dropshipping business.

CHAPTER 5: PRODUCT SOURCING AND SUPPLIER MANAGEMENT

5.1 Product Sourcing Strategies

When it comes to dropshipping, finding reliable suppliers and sourcing quality products at competitive prices is essential. Here are some effective strategies to help you with product sourcing:

1. Supplier Directories: Utilize online supplier directories such as Alibaba, AliExpress, or Oberlo to discover a wide range of products and potential suppliers. These directories provide comprehensive information about suppliers, including their product offerings, pricing, and customer reviews.

2. Trade Shows and Exhibitions: Attend industry trade shows and exhibitions to connect with manufacturers, wholesalers, and distributors directly. This allows you to establish personal relationships, negotiate deals, and assess the quality of products firsthand.

3. Local Sourcing: Explore local sourcing options by reaching out to local manufacturers and wholesalers in your area. This can

offer advantages such as faster shipping times, better control over product quality, and potential cost savings.

4. Supplier Research and Verification: Before partnering with a supplier, conduct thorough research to ensure their reliability and reputation. Look for indicators such as positive customer reviews, prompt communication, and a history of successful partnerships.

5. Product Samples: Request product samples from potential suppliers to assess their quality, packaging, and overall customer experience. This will help you make informed decisions and ensure that the products meet your standards.

6. Niche-Specific Platforms: Explore niche-specific platforms and marketplaces that cater to your target audience. These platforms often have curated selections of products that align with specific niches, making it easier to find suitable suppliers.

5.2 Supplier Management Best Practices

Building and maintaining strong relationships with your suppliers is crucial for the smooth operation of your dropshipping business. Here are some best practices for effective supplier management:

1. Clear Communication: Establish open and transparent communication channels with your suppliers. Clearly communicate your expectations, order requirements, and any specific instructions. Promptly address any concerns or issues that may arise.

2. Consistent Order Monitoring: Regularly monitor the status of your orders to ensure timely processing and shipping. Stay in touch with your suppliers to track inventory levels, address any stock shortages, and maintain a seamless fulfillment process.

3. Quality Control: Implement quality control measures to ensure that the products meet your standards. This may include inspecting product samples, requesting certifications or documentation, or conducting periodic quality checks.

4. Timely Payments: Honor your financial commitments by making timely payments to your suppliers. This helps build trust and strengthens your supplier relationships. Consider setting up automated payment systems to streamline the payment process.

5. Continuous Supplier Evaluation: Regularly assess your suppliers based on their performance, reliability, and customer feedback. Consider factors such as product quality, shipping times, responsiveness, and overall professionalism. If necessary, be prepared to make changes to your supplier lineup to optimize your operations.

6. Nurture Long-Term Partnerships: Foster long-term partnerships with reliable and trustworthy suppliers. Building strong relationships can lead to preferential treatment, better pricing, and improved collaboration opportunities.

By implementing effective product sourcing strategies and adopting best practices for supplier management, you can ensure a consistent supply of quality products to meet customer demands.

CHAPTER 6: CREATING AN EFFECTIVE PRODUCT LISTING

6.1 The Power of Product Listings

Your product listings serve as the virtual storefront for your dropshipping business. They are the primary way to showcase your products, entice customers, and drive conversions. Here are key elements and strategies to create compelling and effective product listings:

1. Captivating Product Titles: Craft attention-grabbing and descriptive titles that highlight the key features and benefits of your products. Use relevant keywords that resonate with your target audience and improve search engine visibility.

2. High-Quality Product Images: Include high-resolution images that accurately represent your products. Use multiple images from different angles, showcasing the product's details and variations. Ensure that the images are visually appealing and professional.

3. Detailed Product Descriptions: Write detailed and persuasive product descriptions that provide comprehensive information

about the product. Highlight its features, specifications, uses, and benefits. Use persuasive language and storytelling techniques to engage potential buyers.

4. Clear Pricing and Special Offers: Clearly display the price of your product, any discounts or special offers, and any additional costs such as shipping or taxes. Be transparent about pricing to build trust and avoid any surprises during the checkout process.

5. Product Variations and Options: If your product comes in different variations, sizes, or colors, clearly present the available options. Use dropdown menus or selection boxes to make it easy for customers to choose their preferred variation.

6. Social Proof and Customer Reviews: Showcase customer reviews and testimonials to provide social proof of your product's quality and value. Positive reviews build trust and encourage potential buyers to make a purchase. Consider implementing a review system and encouraging customers to leave feedback.

7. Clear Call-to-Action Buttons: Place clear and prominent call-to-action buttons such as "Add to Cart" or "Buy Now" near the product information. Make it easy for customers to take the desired action and complete the purchase.

8. SEO Optimization: Incorporate relevant keywords throughout your product listings to improve search engine optimization. Use keyword research tools to identify popular search terms related to your products and include them naturally in your titles and descriptions.

6.2 Product Listing Optimization Techniques

To maximize the effectiveness of your product listings, consider the following optimization techniques:

1. A/B Testing: Experiment with different product titles, images, descriptions, and pricing strategies to determine what resonates best with your target audience. Conduct A/B tests to compare the performance of different elements and optimize your listings based on the results.

2. Keyword Research: Conduct thorough keyword research to identify the most relevant and high-performing keywords for your product listings. Use tools like Google Keyword Planner, SEMrush, or Moz Keyword Explorer to find popular keywords with low competition.

3. Competitive Analysis: Analyze the product listings of your competitors to identify areas for improvement and gain insights into successful strategies. Look for ways to differentiate your listings by highlighting unique selling points or offering additional value.

4. Mobile Optimization: Ensure that your product listings are optimized for mobile devices. With the increasing use of smartphones for online shopping, it's crucial to provide a seamless browsing and purchasing experience for mobile users.

5. Persuasive Copywriting: Use persuasive and engaging language in your product descriptions to evoke emotions, create desire, and convince potential buyers of the value of your products. Incorporate storytelling techniques and address the pain points or needs of your target audience.

6. Visual Enhancements: Consider using visual enhancements such as icons, badges, or labels to draw attention to key product features or benefits. These visual cues can help customers quickly understand the value proposition of your products.

7. Cross-Selling and Upselling Opportunities: Explore opportunities to cross-sell or upsell related products within your product listings. Showcase complementary items or upgrades that enhance the customer's experience or offer additional value.

By implementing these

strategies and optimization techniques, you can create persuasive and compelling product listings that capture the attention of potential buyers, generate interest, and ultimately drive conversions. In the next chapter, we will explore about how to manage inventory and order fulfillment. Stay tuned for valuable insights and tactics to take your dropshipping business to new heights.

CHAPTER 7: MANAGING INVENTORY AND ORDER FULFILLMENT

7.1 Importance of Effective Inventory Management

Efficient inventory management is crucial for the success of your dropshipping business. It ensures that you have sufficient stock to fulfill customer orders promptly, minimizes the risk of stockouts, and optimizes your overall operational efficiency. Here are key strategies for managing your inventory effectively:

1. Accurate Inventory Tracking: Implement a robust inventory tracking system that allows you to monitor stock levels in real-time. This helps you stay informed about the availability of each product and make data-driven decisions regarding restocking.

2. Regular Inventory Audits: Conduct periodic inventory audits to reconcile physical stock with your recorded inventory levels. This helps identify discrepancies, such as damaged or missing items, and allows for timely adjustments.

3. Set Reorder Points: Determine reorder points for each product based on historical sales data and lead times from suppliers. When

the stock level reaches the reorder point, it serves as a trigger to initiate the restocking process.

4. Establish Safety Stock Levels: Maintain a safety stock of popular or high-demand products to mitigate the risk of stockouts during unexpected surges in sales or delays in restocking. This buffer stock provides a safety net to fulfill orders promptly.

5. Supplier Communication: Maintain open and proactive communication with your suppliers regarding inventory levels, restocking timelines, and any potential issues. This ensures that you can align your inventory management with their availability and minimize any disruptions.

6. Dropshipping Automation Tools: Leverage automation tools and software specifically designed for dropshipping to streamline inventory management processes. These tools can help automate order processing, track stock levels, and even facilitate automatic order placement with suppliers.

7.2 Efficient Order Fulfillment Process

Smooth and efficient order fulfillment is crucial for customer satisfaction and repeat business. Here are strategies to optimize your order fulfillment process:

1. Streamlined Order Processing: Implement an efficient order processing system to handle incoming orders seamlessly. This includes automating order confirmation emails, generating packing slips, and updating order status in real-time.

2. Integration with Suppliers: If possible, integrate your e-commerce platform with your suppliers' systems to automate order placement and fulfillment. This minimizes manual intervention, reduces the risk of errors, and speeds up the

fulfillment process.

3. Timely Order Confirmation: Send order confirmation emails to customers promptly after they place an order. This assures them that their order has been received and provides an estimated delivery timeframe.

4. Shipping and Tracking Information: Provide customers with accurate shipping information and tracking numbers once their order has been shipped. This allows them to track the progress of their package and enhances transparency and trust.

5. Packaging and Branding: Pay attention to the packaging of your products to create a positive unboxing experience for customers. Consider including branded materials, personalized notes, or promotional inserts to enhance the overall customer experience.

6. Addressing Returns and Exchanges: Establish clear policies and procedures for handling returns and exchanges. Make the process as convenient as possible for customers while ensuring that it aligns with your business's profitability and sustainability.

7. Customer Support and Communication: Offer responsive customer support to address any inquiries or issues related to order fulfillment promptly. Maintain open lines of communication and provide updates to customers if there are any delays or complications.

By implementing effective inventory management techniques and optimizing your order fulfillment process, you can ensure a seamless and efficient operation for your dropshipping business. In the next chapter, we will explore how to optimise you website for maximum conversion to drive traffic to your store and increase your customer base. Stay tuned for valuable insights and techniques to take your dropshipping business to new heights.

CHAPTER 8: OPTIMIZING YOUR WEBSITE FOR CONVERSIONS

8.1 The Importance of Conversion Optimization

To maximize the success of your dropshipping business, it is essential to optimize your website for conversions. Conversion optimization focuses on improving the user experience, increasing engagement, and ultimately driving more visitors to complete desired actions, such as making a purchase or subscribing to your newsletter. Here are key strategies to optimize your website for conversions:

1. Clear and Intuitive Navigation: Ensure that your website has a clear and intuitive navigation structure. Organize your product categories, pages, and links in a logical manner, making it easy for visitors to find what they are looking for. Use descriptive labels and minimize the number of clicks required to access important information.

2. Streamlined Checkout Process: Simplify your checkout process to reduce friction and increase the likelihood of completing a purchase. Minimize the number of steps and form fields required, offer guest checkout options, and provide clear instructions

throughout the process. Implement trusted payment gateways and security badges to instill confidence in your customers.

3. Mobile-Friendly Design: Optimize your website for mobile devices to cater to the growing number of users accessing the internet through smartphones and tablets. Ensure that your website is responsive, loads quickly, and offers a seamless browsing experience across different screen sizes.

4. High-Quality Visuals: Utilize high-quality product images and videos to showcase your products in the best possible light. Use professional photography, multiple angles, and zoom features to allow visitors to examine the details of your products. Incorporate lifestyle images that demonstrate product use and create a sense of desire.

5. Persuasive Call-to-Action Buttons: Use compelling and prominently placed call-to-action (CTA) buttons throughout your website to guide visitors towards desired actions. Use persuasive language such as "Add to Cart," "Buy Now," or "Subscribe" to encourage conversions. Experiment with different button colors, sizes, and placements to determine what works best for your audience.

6. Clear Product Descriptions: Craft clear and concise product descriptions that highlight the unique selling points and benefits of your products. Use bullet points, headings, and formatting to make the information easy to scan. Incorporate customer reviews and testimonials to provide social proof and build trust.

7. Trust Signals: Display trust signals throughout your website to establish credibility and alleviate any concerns visitors may have. Include customer reviews and ratings, security badges, SSL certificates, and any industry affiliations or certifications you

possess. Highlight any free shipping, money-back guarantee, or hassle-free return policies to instill confidence in potential buyers.

8. Speed and Performance Optimization: Optimize your website's loading speed and performance to provide a smooth and fast browsing experience. Compress images, minify CSS and JavaScript files, leverage caching, and utilize a reliable hosting provider to ensure your website loads quickly. Slow-loading websites can lead to high bounce rates and lost conversions.

8.2 Testing and Optimization Techniques

To continually improve your website's conversion rates, employ the following testing and optimization techniques:

1. A/B Testing: Conduct A/B tests by creating variations of specific elements on your website, such as headlines, CTA buttons, or product images. Split your traffic between the original and variant versions and measure the impact on conversion rates. Implement the changes that result in higher conversions.

2. Heatmap Analysis: Utilize heatmap tools to gain insights into user behavior on your website. Heatmaps visually represent the areas where users click, scroll, or spend the most time. Analyze the data to identify potential areas of improvement and make informed design and content decisions.

3. Conversion Funnel Analysis: Analyze your website's conversion funnel to identify potential bottlenecks or areas of drop-off. Use analytics tools to track user behavior from landing page to

conversion and pinpoint areas where

users are exiting the funnel. Make adjustments to improve the flow and reduce friction.

4. User Feedback and Surveys: Collect user feedback through surveys, live chat, or customer support interactions. Ask visitors about their experience on your website, what challenges they encountered, and any suggestions they may have. Use this feedback to identify pain points and make targeted improvements.

5. Personalization and Dynamic Content: Implement personalization techniques to tailor the website experience based on user preferences, behavior, or demographics. Show relevant product recommendations, offer personalized discounts, or display dynamic content based on the visitor's location or browsing history. Personalization can enhance engagement and increase conversions.

By implementing these strategies and optimization techniques, you can create a website that not only attracts visitors but also encourages them to take action. In the next chapter, we will explore different marketing strategies for dropshipping business. Stay tuned for valuable insights and techniques to take your dropshipping business to new heights.

CHAPTER 9: MARKETING STRATEGIES FOR DROPSHIPPING SUCCESS

9.1 The Importance of Effective Marketing

Marketing plays a pivotal role in the success of your dropshipping business. It helps you reach your target audience, build brand awareness, and drive traffic to your website. By implementing effective marketing strategies, you can generate leads, increase conversions, and ultimately boost your sales. Here are key marketing strategies for dropshipping success:

1. Search Engine Optimization (SEO): Optimize your website and product pages for search engines to improve your organic visibility. Conduct keyword research to identify relevant and high-volume search terms, and incorporate them naturally into your content. Focus on on-page optimization, meta tags, and building high-quality backlinks to improve your search engine rankings.

2. Pay-Per-Click Advertising (PPC): Consider using PPC advertising

platforms like Google Ads or Bing Ads to display targeted ads to potential customers. Set up strategic campaigns based on relevant keywords, demographics, and geographic locations. Monitor and optimize your ads to maximize your return on investment (ROI).

3. Social Media Marketing: Leverage the power of social media platforms to reach and engage with your target audience. Create compelling content, including images, videos, and blog posts, to share across platforms like Facebook, Instagram, Twitter, and Pinterest. Use social media advertising options to target specific demographics and promote your products.

4. Influencer Marketing: Collaborate with influencers who have a strong presence and influence within your target market. They can promote your products to their followers through sponsored posts, reviews, or giveaways. Identify influencers whose values align with your brand and whose audience matches your target customer profile.

5. Content Marketing: Develop a content marketing strategy to provide valuable and informative content related to your products or niche. Create blog posts, articles, tutorials, and videos that address your audience's pain points, offer solutions, and establish you as an authority in your industry. Optimize your content for search engines and share it across relevant platforms to attract and engage potential customers.

6. Email Marketing: Build an email list of interested prospects and existing customers to nurture relationships and drive sales. Send regular newsletters, personalized product recommendations, exclusive offers, and updates about new arrivals or promotions. Use email automation tools to segment your list and deliver targeted messages.

7. Affiliate Marketing: Establish an affiliate program where you partner with affiliates who promote your products in exchange for a commission on sales. Provide them with promotional materials, unique affiliate links, and tracking tools to monitor their performance. This allows you to expand your reach and tap into the networks of affiliates who have their own audiences.

8. Retargeting and Remarketing: Implement retargeting strategies to reach out to users who have visited your website but have not made a purchase. Display targeted ads to them on other platforms they frequent, reminding them of the products they showed interest in. Use email remarketing by sending follow-up emails to potential customers who abandoned their carts.

9. Collaborations and Partnerships: Seek collaborations and partnerships with complementary businesses or influencers in your industry. This can include co-hosting events, cross-promotions, or joint marketing campaigns. By leveraging each other's audience and networks, you can expand your reach and attract new customers.

9.2 Analytics and Optimization

To measure the effectiveness of your marketing efforts and optimize your strategies, utilize analytics tools and techniques:

1. Website Analytics: Set up tools like Google Analytics to track website traffic, user behavior, and conversion rates. Analyze the data to identify trends, popular pages, and areas for improvement. Use this information to make data-driven decisions and refine your marketing strategies.

2. Conversion Tracking: Implement conversion tracking on your website to monitor the performance of different marketing

channels and campaigns. This allows you to allocate your marketing budget effectively and optimize campaigns that drive the highest conversions.

3. A/B Testing: Conduct A/B tests on different elements of your marketing campaigns, such as ad copies, landing page designs, or email subject lines. Compare the performance of different variations and implement changes based on the results.

4. Customer Surveys and Feedback: Collect feedback from your customers to gain insights into their preferences, satisfaction levels, and suggestions for improvement. Use this feedback to refine your marketing strategies and enhance the overall customer experience.

By implementing these marketing strategies and utilizing analytics for optimization, you can effectively promote your dropshipping business, attract your target audience, and drive conversions. In the next chapter, we will explore about social media marketing and influencer marketing. Stay tuned for valuable insights and techniques to take your dropshipping business to new heights.

CHAPTER 10: SOCIAL MEDIA ADVERTISING AND INFLUENCER MARKETING

10.1 Leveraging Social Media Advertising

Social media platforms have become powerful channels for advertising and reaching a wide audience. By leveraging social media advertising, you can effectively promote your dropshipping business and target specific demographics. Here are key strategies for successful social media advertising:

1. Define Your Objectives: Clearly define your advertising objectives, whether it's increasing brand awareness, driving website traffic, or generating direct sales. This will help you choose the right social media platforms and create compelling ad campaigns that align with your goals.

2. Choose the Right Platforms: Identify the social media platforms where your target audience is most active. Consider platforms like Facebook, Instagram, Twitter, LinkedIn, or Pinterest. Each platform has its unique features, demographics, and advertising

options, so choose the ones that best align with your target market.

3. Audience Targeting: Take advantage of the advanced targeting options offered by social media advertising platforms. Define your audience based on demographics, interests, behaviors, and location. This allows you to deliver your ads to the most relevant audience, increasing the chances of engagement and conversions.

4. Compelling Ad Creative: Create visually appealing and engaging ad creative that captures the attention of users scrolling through their social media feeds. Use high-quality images or videos that showcase your products or convey your brand message effectively. Craft compelling ad copy that highlights the benefits of your products and includes a strong call-to-action.

5. Ad Testing and Optimization: Conduct A/B testing to experiment with different variations of your ads. Test different visuals, ad copy, headlines, and call-to-action buttons to determine which combinations yield the best results. Monitor the performance of your ads and optimize them based on key metrics such as click-through rates, conversion rates, and return on ad spend.

6. Retargeting Campaigns: Implement retargeting campaigns to re-engage users who have shown interest in your products but have not made a purchase. Set up pixels or tracking codes on your website to track user behavior, and then display targeted ads to these users on social media platforms. This can help remind them of your products and encourage them to complete their purchase.

10.2 Influencer Marketing

Influencer marketing has gained significant traction in recent years and can be a valuable strategy for promoting your dropshipping business. Collaborating with influencers allows you to tap into their engaged audience and benefit from their trust and influence. Here's how to effectively leverage influencer marketing:

1. Define Your Influencer Criteria: Determine the type of influencers that align with your brand and target audience. Look for influencers whose values, content style, and audience demographics match your target market. Consider factors such as their follower count, engagement rates, and relevance to your niche.

2. Research and Identify Influencers: Conduct thorough research to find influencers in your industry or niche. Utilize social media platforms, influencer marketing platforms, or engage the services of influencer marketing agencies to identify suitable influencers. Evaluate their content quality, engagement rates, audience authenticity, and previous brand collaborations.

3. Building Relationships: Approach influencers with a personalized and genuine outreach message. Showcase your understanding of their content and express your interest in collaborating. Offer a value proposition, whether it's monetary compensation, free products, or exclusive discounts for their audience. Building a strong relationship with influencers can lead to long-term partnerships and mutual benefits.

4. Campaign Collaboration: Collaborate with influencers to create authentic and engaging sponsored content that promotes your products. Provide clear guidelines and creative direction, but also allow room for their creativity and unique storytelling. Encourage them to share their honest experiences and opinions to maintain authenticity and build trust with their audience.

5. Track and Measure Results: Set up tracking mechanisms to measure the effectiveness of your influencer campaigns. Track key metrics such as engagement

rates, website traffic, conversions, and ROI. Evaluate the performance of each influencer and their impact on your overall marketing objectives. Use these insights to refine your future influencer marketing strategies.

Social media advertising and influencer marketing can significantly amplify your reach and generate brand awareness for your dropshipping business. By strategically leveraging these channels, you can connect with your target audience, drive traffic to your website, and ultimately increase conversions and sales. In the next chapter, we will delve into search engine optimization (SEO) for E-commers. Stay tuned for valuable insights and techniques to excel in customer satisfaction.

CHAPTER 11: SEARCH ENGINE OPTIMIZATION (SEO) FOR E-COMMERCE

11.1 Understanding the Importance of SEO for E-commerce

Search Engine Optimization (SEO) is a critical aspect of running a successful e-commerce business. It involves optimizing your website and product pages to rank higher in search engine results, driving organic traffic and increasing visibility. By implementing effective SEO strategies, you can attract more potential customers and improve your overall online presence. Here's what you need to know about SEO for e-commerce:

1. Increased Visibility: When your website ranks higher in search engine results, it becomes more visible to users searching for relevant products or services. This increased visibility can lead to higher organic traffic, as users are more likely to click on websites listed on the first page of search results.

2. Targeted Traffic: SEO helps you attract targeted traffic to your e-commerce website. By optimizing your website for specific

keywords related to your products or niche, you can reach users who are actively searching for those items. This targeted traffic has a higher likelihood of converting into customers.

3. Trust and Credibility: Websites that rank higher in search results are often perceived as more trustworthy and credible by users. When your website appears on the first page of search results, it instills confidence in potential customers and increases the likelihood of them making a purchase.

4. Long-Term Benefits: SEO is a long-term strategy that can provide ongoing benefits for your e-commerce business. Once you achieve higher rankings, it becomes easier to maintain them with consistent efforts. Unlike paid advertising, which stops generating traffic once the campaign ends, SEO continues to drive organic traffic over time.

11.2 SEO Strategies for E-commerce Success

To optimize your e-commerce website for search engines, consider implementing the following strategies:

1. Keyword Research: Conduct thorough keyword research to identify the most relevant and high-volume keywords for your e-commerce business. Focus on long-tail keywords that have lower competition but higher intent. Incorporate these keywords naturally into your product titles, descriptions, headings, and content.

2. On-Page Optimization: Optimize your website's on-page elements to improve its search engine visibility. This includes optimizing meta tags (title tags and meta descriptions) with

relevant keywords, using descriptive URLs, and structuring your content with headings (H1, H2, etc.). Ensure your product pages have unique and compelling descriptions that highlight their features, benefits, and unique selling points.

3. Site Speed Optimization: Page loading speed is a crucial factor in SEO and user experience. Optimize your website's loading speed by compressing images, leveraging browser caching, and minimizing unnecessary scripts or plugins. A faster website not only improves search engine rankings but also enhances user satisfaction and reduces bounce rates.

4. Mobile-Friendly Design: With the increasing use of mobile devices for online shopping, having a mobile-friendly website is essential. Ensure your e-commerce website is responsive and optimized for different screen sizes. This improves user experience and can positively impact your search engine rankings, as mobile-friendliness is a ranking factor.

5. High-Quality Content: Create informative, unique, and high-quality content that is relevant to your products and target audience. Develop a blog or resource section where you can publish articles, guides, or tutorials related to your industry or niche. Engaging content not only attracts organic traffic but also encourages backlinks from other reputable websites.

6. User-Generated Content: Encourage customers to leave reviews and ratings for the products they purchase. User-generated content adds credibility to your website and helps improve search engine rankings. Implement a review system and showcase customer testimonials to build trust and enhance the overall user experience.

7. Link Building: Earn backlinks from authoritative and relevant

websites to improve your website's domain authority. Reach out to other websites, bloggers, or influencers in your industry

and offer them valuable content or collaboration opportunities. Guest blogging, influencer partnerships, and participation in industry events can help you build a strong backlink profile.

8. Monitoring and Analytics: Regularly monitor your website's performance using analytics tools such as Google Analytics. Track important metrics like organic traffic, keyword rankings, conversion rates, and bounce rates. Analyze the data to identify areas for improvement and adjust your SEO strategies accordingly.

Implementing these SEO strategies will help your e-commerce website rank higher in search engine results, increase organic traffic, and ultimately drive more sales. In the next chapter, we will explore Email marketing and customer retention. Stay tuned for valuable insights and techniques to maintain a positive brand image and customer satisfaction.

CHAPTER 12: EMAIL MARKETING AND CUSTOMER RETENTION

12.1 The Power of Email Marketing for Customer Retention

Email marketing is a highly effective strategy for customer retention in the world of e-commerce. It allows you to engage with your existing customers, build stronger relationships, and encourage repeat purchases. By leveraging email marketing, you can nurture customer loyalty and increase customer lifetime value. Here's how to make the most of email marketing for customer retention:

1. Welcome Emails: Send a warm and personalized welcome email to new customers as soon as they make a purchase or sign up for your newsletter. Use this opportunity to express your appreciation, introduce your brand values, and provide relevant information about your products or services. Consider offering a special discount or incentive as a token of gratitude.

2. Personalized Product Recommendations: Utilize customer

data and purchase history to provide personalized product recommendations via email. Tailor your recommendations based on their previous purchases, browsing behavior, or demographic information. Highlight products that complement their previous purchases or showcase new arrivals that align with their interests.

3. Exclusive Offers and Promotions: Reward your loyal customers with exclusive offers and promotions through email campaigns. Provide special discounts, early access to sales, or limited-time offers. Make customers feel valued and appreciated by offering them exclusive benefits that are not available to the general public.

4. Abandoned Cart Recovery: Implement automated emails to remind customers who have abandoned their shopping carts to complete their purchase. Send a series of emails with persuasive messaging, emphasizing the benefits of the products and offering incentives like free shipping or a discount. This gentle reminder can significantly increase cart conversion rates.

5. Post-Purchase Follow-up: Show your customers that you care about their satisfaction by sending post-purchase follow-up emails. Thank them for their purchase, ask for feedback or product reviews, and provide additional resources or support. This demonstrates your commitment to their happiness and helps build a lasting relationship.

6. Customer Surveys and Feedback: Send email surveys to gather feedback from your customers about their experience with your products, services, and overall shopping journey. Use their feedback to improve your offerings, address any concerns, and enhance the customer experience. Showing that you value their opinion can strengthen the bond with your customers.

7. Seasonal and Holiday Campaigns: Leverage seasonal or holiday occasions to create targeted email campaigns. Offer special promotions, gift ideas, or curated collections that align with the theme of the season. Tailor your messaging to evoke a sense of excitement and exclusivity, encouraging customers to engage with your brand during these periods.

12.2 Best Practices for Effective Email Marketing

To ensure the success of your email marketing campaigns, follow these best practices:

1. Build a Segmented Email List: Segment your email list based on customer demographics, purchase history, or engagement levels. This allows you to send more personalized and relevant content to different customer segments, increasing the chances of engagement and conversions.

2. Engaging Subject Lines: Craft compelling subject lines that grab attention and entice recipients to open your emails. Use personalization, urgency, or curiosity to create a sense of intrigue. However, avoid using misleading or spammy subject lines, as it can harm your brand reputation.

3. Mobile-Optimized Design: Optimize your email designs for mobile devices, as a significant portion of emails are accessed through smartphones or tablets. Ensure your emails are responsive, visually appealing, and easy to navigate on smaller screens.

4. Clear Call-to-Action (CTA): Include a clear and prominent call-to-action (CTA) in your emails. Whether it's directing customers to a product page, encouraging them to make a purchase, or

inviting them to engage with your content, the CTA should be noticeable and compelling.

5. A/B Testing: Experiment with different elements of your email campaigns using

A/B testing. Test variations in subject lines, email content, CTA placement, or design to identify what resonates best with your audience. Analyze the results and optimize your campaigns based on the insights gained.

6. Email Automation: Utilize automation tools to streamline your email marketing efforts. Set up automated workflows for welcome emails, abandoned cart recovery, or post-purchase follow-ups. This saves time and ensures timely communication with your customers.

7. Monitor and Analyze Performance: Regularly monitor the performance of your email campaigns using analytics. Track open rates, click-through rates, conversion rates, and unsubscribe rates. Analyze the data to identify trends, areas for improvement, and opportunities to enhance your email marketing strategy.

By implementing these email marketing strategies and best practices, you can effectively engage with your customers, nurture their loyalty, and increase their likelihood of repeat purchases.

CHAPTER 13: CUSTOMER SERVICE AND HANDLING RETURNS

13.1 The Importance of Exceptional Customer Service

In the dropshipping business, providing exceptional customer service is paramount to building trust, fostering loyalty, and ensuring customer satisfaction. Positive customer experiences not only lead to repeat purchases but also generate positive word-of-mouth and referrals. Here are key strategies for delivering outstanding customer service:

1. Prompt and Responsive Communication: Establish clear and efficient communication channels with your customers. Respond to customer inquiries and concerns promptly, addressing them in a professional and courteous manner. Offer multiple contact options such as email, live chat, or phone support, and clearly display this information on your website.

2. Knowledgeable and Empathetic Support Team: Train your customer support team to be knowledgeable about your products, policies, and order processes. Empower them to resolve customer issues effectively and efficiently. Encourage active listening,

empathy, and problem-solving skills to ensure a positive customer interaction.

3. Timely Order Fulfillment: Ensure timely order fulfillment to meet customer expectations. Communicate accurate shipping times and provide tracking information. Proactively notify customers about any delays or issues with their orders and offer solutions or alternatives to mitigate their concerns.

4. Hassle-Free Returns and Exchanges: Establish a clear and customer-friendly return and exchange policy. Make the process easy and straightforward for customers who wish to return or exchange their products. Provide clear instructions and offer prompt refunds or replacements upon receiving returned items.

5. Personalization and Individual Attention: Treat each customer as an individual and provide personalized assistance whenever possible. Address customers by their names and reference their previous interactions or purchase history. Offer product recommendations based on their preferences, and provide relevant and targeted information to enhance their shopping experience.

6. Proactive Customer Feedback: Regularly seek feedback from your customers to gauge their satisfaction levels and identify areas for improvement. Send post-purchase surveys or follow-up emails to gather insights about their experience. Actively listen to their feedback and take necessary steps to address any issues or suggestions raised.

13.2 Effective Handling of Returns and Exchanges

Returns and exchanges are inevitable in the e-commerce business. It is essential to have a well-defined process in place to handle these situations effectively. Here's how you can navigate returns and exchanges with professionalism and efficiency:

1. Clear Return Policy: Clearly outline your return and exchange policy on your website. Include information about the timeframe for returns, acceptable reasons, and any additional requirements or conditions. Make sure this information is easily accessible and prominently displayed.

2. Streamlined Return Process: Create a streamlined and user-friendly return process. Provide clear instructions on how customers can initiate a return or exchange, including any required documentation or forms. Consider offering prepaid return labels or arranging for pickup services to make the process more convenient for customers.

3. Efficient Returns Handling: Once a return is initiated, promptly acknowledge the request and provide instructions on how to proceed. Upon receiving the returned item, inspect it for damage or defects. Process refunds or exchanges in a timely manner, keeping the customer informed at every step of the process.

4. Learn from Returns: Use returns as an opportunity to gather valuable feedback and improve your products or processes. Analyze the reasons for returns and identify any recurring issues or patterns. Use this information to make necessary adjustments, whether it's improving product descriptions, enhancing packaging, or addressing quality concerns.

5. Exemplary Customer Service: Even in the case of returns or exchanges, continue to provide exceptional customer service. Be understanding, empathetic, and responsive to customers' concerns. Resolve any issues promptly and ensure that the customer feels valued throughout the process.

By prioritizing exceptional customer service and handling returns and exchanges efficiently, you can build trust and loyalty among your customers. In the next chapter, we will exploring about scaling your dropshipping business.

CHAPTER 14: SCALING YOUR DROPSHIPPING BUSINESS

14.1 The Importance of Scaling

As your dropshipping business grows, it becomes crucial to scale your operations to meet increasing demands. Scaling allows you to maximize your profits, reach a wider audience, and take advantage of new opportunities. However, scaling requires careful planning and execution to ensure continued success. Here are key strategies for scaling your dropshipping business effectively:

1. Review and Optimize Your Processes: Before scaling, review your existing processes and identify areas for improvement. Streamline your order fulfillment, inventory management, and customer support processes to increase efficiency and reduce errors. Automation tools and software can help streamline and optimize various aspects of your operations.

2. Expand Your Product Range: Consider expanding your product range to cater to a broader customer base. Research market trends, analyze customer preferences, and identify potential new products or product categories to add to your inventory. Ensure that these products align with your brand and target market.

3. Establish Strong Supplier Relationships: Strengthen your relationships with reliable suppliers to ensure a consistent and high-quality supply of products. Negotiate favorable terms, such as bulk discounts or priority access to new products. Collaborate closely with your suppliers to manage inventory levels effectively and minimize stockouts.

4. Invest in Marketing and Advertising: Increase your marketing efforts to reach a larger audience and drive more traffic to your website. Invest in paid advertising channels such as social media ads, search engine marketing, or influencer partnerships. Implement effective search engine optimization (SEO) strategies to improve your organic visibility and attract organic traffic.

5. Enhance Customer Experience: Focus on providing an exceptional customer experience to foster loyalty and drive repeat purchases. Continuously improve your website design, user interface, and navigation to create a seamless and user-friendly shopping experience. Personalize communication, offer excellent customer support, and leverage customer feedback to enhance your services.

6. Leverage Data and Analytics: Utilize data and analytics to gain insights into customer behavior, sales trends, and marketing effectiveness. Monitor key performance indicators (KPIs) such as conversion rates, average order value, and customer lifetime value. Analyze the data to make data-driven decisions, identify growth opportunities, and optimize your marketing and sales strategies.

7. Explore New Sales Channels: Consider expanding beyond your existing sales channels to reach a wider audience. Explore additional online marketplaces, such as Amazon or eBay, or establish partnerships with brick-and-mortar retailers to expand

your reach. Evaluate the feasibility of international markets and explore opportunities for global expansion.

14.2 Managing Growth Challenges

Scaling your dropshipping business also comes with challenges that need to be effectively managed. Here are some common challenges and strategies to overcome them:

1. Inventory Management: As your business scales, managing inventory becomes more complex. Implement inventory management systems and software to track stock levels, monitor product performance, and automate reordering processes. Establish effective communication channels with your suppliers to ensure timely replenishment.

2. Operational Efficiency: Maintain operational efficiency as you scale by continuously optimizing your processes. Identify bottlenecks, invest in automation tools, and streamline workflows to handle increasing order volumes without sacrificing quality or customer satisfaction.

3. Customer Support: Scaling can place a strain on customer support resources. Invest in customer support tools and software to streamline communication and efficiently handle customer inquiries. Consider outsourcing customer support or hiring additional staff to ensure prompt and effective support.

4. Cash Flow Management: Scaling requires upfront investments in inventory, marketing, and infrastructure. Monitor and manage your cash flow effectively to ensure sufficient funds to support growth. Seek funding options if needed, such as loans or investors, to fuel expansion and manage cash flow gaps.

5. Competitive Landscape: As your business grows, competition may intensify. Stay competitive by continuously monitoring the market, understanding your competitors' strategies, and differentiating your brand

through unique value propositions, exceptional customer service, or exclusive product offerings.

6. Scalable Technology Infrastructure: Ensure that your technology infrastructure can handle the increased demands of a scaled business. Invest in scalable hosting, robust e-commerce platforms, and secure payment gateways to support increased traffic, transactions, and data management.

Scaling your dropshipping business requires careful planning, strategic decision-making, and continuous adaptation. Monitor market trends, customer preferences, and industry developments to identify opportunities for growth and expansion. By effectively scaling your business, you can achieve long-term success and establish a strong position in the competitive e-commerce landscape.

In the final chapter of our book, we will discuss the future of dropshipping and explore emerging trends and technologies that are shaping the industry. Stay tuned for valuable insights on staying ahead in the ever-evolving world of dropshipping.

CHAPTER 15: LEGAL CONSIDERATIONS AND FUTURE TRENDS

15.1 Legal Considerations for Dropshipping Businesses

Operating a dropshipping business entails various legal considerations to ensure compliance and protect your business. Here are some key legal aspects to consider:

1. Business Structure: Determine the appropriate business structure for your dropshipping business, such as a sole proprietorship, partnership, or limited liability company (LLC). Consult with legal professionals or business advisors to choose the structure that offers the best liability protection and tax advantages for your specific situation.

2. Business Licenses and Permits: Research and obtain any necessary business licenses and permits required by your local and regional authorities. These may include general business licenses, sales tax permits, or permits specific to certain industries or products. Compliance with legal requirements is essential to avoid penalties and legal issues.

3. Product Compliance and Safety: Ensure that the products you sell comply with applicable safety standards and regulations.

Familiarize yourself with product labeling requirements, warning labels, and any industry-specific regulations. Stay updated on product recalls and take prompt action if any of your products are affected.

4. Intellectual Property Rights: Respect intellectual property rights and avoid infringing on trademarks, copyrights, or patents. Conduct thorough research to ensure that your branding, product names, and marketing materials do not infringe on existing intellectual property. Consider trademark registration to protect your own brand.

5. Privacy and Data Protection: Protect customer privacy and comply with data protection regulations. Implement privacy policies that clearly outline how customer data is collected, stored, and used. Ensure that you have appropriate security measures in place to safeguard customer information and prevent data breaches.

6. Terms and Conditions: Establish clear terms and conditions for your dropshipping business. Cover important aspects such as payment terms, shipping policies, return and refund policies, and customer obligations. Consult with legal professionals to draft comprehensive and enforceable terms and conditions.

7. Contractual Agreements: Review and negotiate contractual agreements with suppliers, manufacturers, and third-party service providers. Ensure that the agreements clearly define the responsibilities, obligations, and rights of each party. Seek legal advice to ensure that your agreements protect your interests.

15.2 Future Trends in Dropshipping

The dropshipping industry continues to evolve, driven by

technological advancements, changing consumer preferences, and market dynamics. Here are some future trends to watch out for:

1. Diversification of Product Sourcing: Dropshipping businesses are increasingly diversifying their product sourcing strategies. In addition to traditional suppliers, they are exploring partnerships with local manufacturers, artisans, or even creating their own private label brands. This allows for greater control over product quality, differentiation, and exclusivity.

2. Integration of Artificial Intelligence (AI): AI-powered tools and algorithms are becoming integral to dropshipping operations. AI can optimize inventory management, personalize customer experiences, automate pricing strategies, and enhance marketing campaigns. Embracing AI technology can provide a competitive edge and improve efficiency.

3. Sustainable and Ethical Practices: Consumers are increasingly conscious of sustainability and ethical considerations. Dropshipping businesses are responding by focusing on eco-friendly packaging, sustainable sourcing, and supporting ethical manufacturing practices. Incorporating sustainability into your business strategy can attract environmentally-conscious consumers and align with emerging market trends.

4. Augmented Reality (AR) and Virtual Reality (VR): AR and VR technologies are transforming the online shopping experience. By allowing customers to virtually try on products or visualize them in their homes, these technologies enhance engagement and reduce the likelihood of returns. Integrating AR and VR into your website or mobile app can improve customer satisfaction and boost sales.

5. Omnichannel Retailing: Dropshipping businesses are expanding beyond their online stores to establish a presence across multiple channels. This includes selling on popular marketplaces, social media platforms, and even opening physical retail locations. Adopting an omnichannel approach

provides wider reach and convenience for customers.

6. Voice Commerce: With the rise of smart speakers and virtual assistants, voice commerce is gaining prominence. Dropshipping businesses are optimizing their websites for voice search and exploring voice-enabled shopping experiences. Voice-activated ordering and personalized recommendations through voice assistants can enhance customer convenience and engagement.

7. Cross-Border Expansion: The globalization of e-commerce presents opportunities for dropshipping businesses to expand into international markets. With the right logistics infrastructure and localization strategies, tapping into new markets can drive growth and diversify revenue streams.

As you navigate the legal landscape and embrace future trends, staying informed and adaptable will be key to the long-term success of your dropshipping business.

Congratulations on reaching the end of our comprehensive book, "The Art of E-commerce: Mastering the Dropshipping Business." We hope the insights and strategies shared throughout the chapters will guide you towards building a successful and thriving dropshipping business. Remember, continuous learning, adaptation, and innovation are essential in the dynamic world of e-commerce. Good luck on your entrepreneurial journey!

www.ingramcontent.com/pod-product-compliance
Lightning Source LLC
Chambersburg PA
CBHW031548210526
45464CB00003B/1206